Presented to

Shadai Kennedy

From

Jean & Jessica Banks Dora

On this date

December 25, 2021

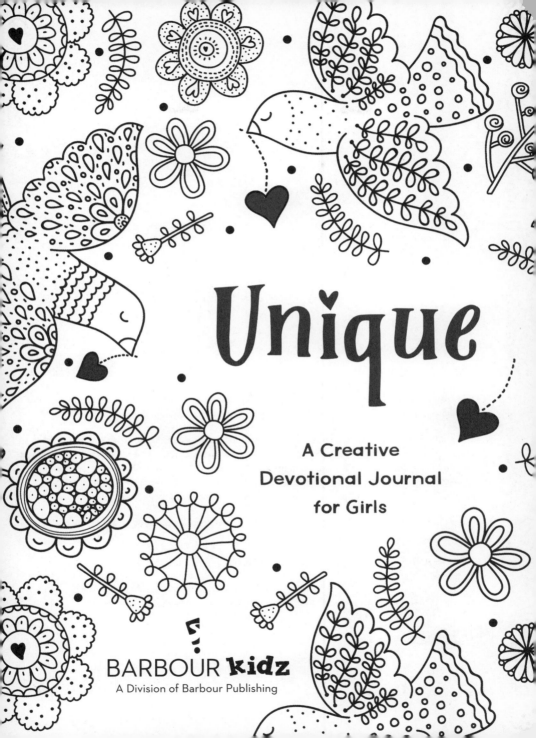

Unique

A Creative Devotional Journal for Girls

BARBOUR **kidz**

A Division of Barbour Publishing

Print ISBN 978-1-63609-017-7

Published by Barbour Publishing, Inc., 1810 Barbour Drive, Uhrichsville, Ohio 44683, www.barbourbooks.com

Our mission is to inspire the world with the life-changing message of the Bible.

Member of the
Evangelical Christian
Publishers Association

Printed in China.

000836   0921   HA

Just a few of the *many* ways God shows His love for me. . .

1) **He made me!**

   You made the parts inside me. You put me together inside my mother.

   —PSALM 139:13

2) **He knows me.**

   God knows how many hairs you have on your head.

   —MATTHEW 10:30

3) **He listens to me.**

   Then you will call upon Me and come and pray to Me, and I will listen to you.

   —JEREMIAH 29:12

4) **He protects me.**

   "Do not be afraid. For I have bought you and made you free. I have called you by name. You are Mine!"

   —ISAIAH 43:1

5) **He comforts me.**

   Do not fear, for I am with you. Do not be afraid, for I am your God. I will give you strength, and for sure I will help you. Yes, I will hold you up with My right hand that is right and good.

   —ISAIAH 41:10

6) **He gives me everything I need.**

   And my God will give you everything you need because of His great riches in Christ Jesus.

   —PHILIPPIANS 4:19

7) **He keeps His promises.**

   Know then that the Lord your God is God, the faithful God. He keeps His promise and shows His loving-kindness to those who love Him.

   —DEUTERONOMY 7:9

8) **He gives me joy**.

And my spirit is happy in God, the One Who saves.

—Luke 1:47

9) **He gives me hope**.

Our hope comes from God. May He fill you with joy and peace because of your trust in Him.

—Romans 15:13

10) **He gives me strength**.

I can do all things because Christ gives me the strength.

—Philippians 4:13

11) **He forgives me**.

It was because of His loving-kindness that He washed our sins away. At the same time He gave us new life when the Holy Spirit came into our lives.

—Titus 3:5

12) **He has a plan for me**.

"For I know the plans I have for you," says the Lord, "plans for well-being and not for trouble, to give you a future and a hope."

—Jeremiah 29:11

13) **He is always with me**.

God has said, "I will never leave you or let you be alone."

—Hebrews 13:5

14) **He offers me eternal life**.

For God so loved the world that He gave His only Son. Whoever puts his trust in God's Son will no be lost but will have life that lasts forever.

—John 3:16

God's amazing love makes me feel like this!

(Draw a picture in the space below.)

For I know that nothing can keep us from the love of God.
ROMANS 8:38

One of a Kind

Have you ever tried to be like someone else? Why do you think it didn't work? Because you are most comfortable being *yourself*!

You are a work of art—created by God Himself! Everything that makes you *you* was chosen by Him! When you try to be like someone else, it's like telling God that He didn't do a good job when He made you. How do you think that makes Him feel?

God wants you to shine as His creation. So quit trying to be like other people. Stand out! Be *yourself*!

In what ways can you "shine" for God?

....

....

....

....

....

....

....

....

....

....

....

....

....

....

....

*We are the clay, and You are our
pot maker. All of us are the
work of Your hand.*
ISAIAH 64:8

God Is Right Here—All the Time!

God loves you, and He wants a special relationship with you. He has promised that if you seek Him with your whole heart, you will find Him.

Spend some time with God today. Talk to Him in prayer. Talk to Him just like you would your best friend—that *is* what He wants to be after all. Then choose a passage from the Bible to read, and let God speak to you.

Seek Him with your heart—you *will* find Him!

What do you need to share with God today? Write your prayer in the space below.

....
....
....
....
....
....
....
....
....
....
....
....
....
....

*From there you will look for the
Lord your God. And you will find
Him if you look for Him with
all your heart and soul.*
DEUTERONOMY 4:29

God Knows You!

Have you ever had a day when everything seems to go wrong? When it seems like no one understands you? And no one knows how you feel?

On those days, remember that the God who created you knows *everything* about you—even how many hairs are on your head! God knows *every* feeling you have—bad and good. And He is *always* there for you.

Take all your hurts to Him in prayer. He will understand and comfort you. No one knows you quite like He does!

How well does God know you?

....

....

....

....

....

....

....

....

....

....

....

....

....

....

....

....

....

*God knows how many hairs
you have on your head.*
MATTHEW 10:30

Never Lonely

Read Psalm 139 in your Bible. God knows *everything* about us. He knows when we sit down and stand up, and He even knows everything we're going to say before we ever say it! *Amazing!* Psalm 139 tells us that no matter where we go. . .as high up as heaven, or to the far side of the sea . . .even in darkness or in light. . .God is always with us *no matter what!*

Remember that God is more than the Creator of all things. . .He is our heavenly Father who knows you and wants to have a relationship with you!

Why is it important to know that God is always with you?

....

....

....

....

....

....

....

....

....

....

....

....

....

....

....

....

....

....

....

You have laid Your hand upon me.
PSALM 139:5

No Worries

Are you a worrier? If so, you're not alone. Lots of people worry—about big things and even silly little things.

But God doesn't want us to worry! Jesus tells His followers in Matthew 6 that true believers should have faith and trust that God will always give us what we need.

So the next time you begin to have worrisome thoughts, remind yourself that God already knows your needs. And He's taking care of them right now!

Make a list of all the things God has provided for you.

....
....
....
....
....
....
....
....
....
....
....
....
....
....
....

"Do not worry. Do not keep saying, 'What will we eat?' or, 'What will we drink?' or, 'What will we wear?' The people who do not know God are looking for all these things. Your Father in heaven knows you need all these things. First of all, look for the holy nation of God. Be right with Him. All these other things will be given to you also."
MATTHEW 6:31–33

Your Best

Have you ever been tempted to do the least amount of work you can just to get by—without giving your very best?

It's true that God has given each of us special gifts and talents, but this doesn't mean we should never work hard at other things. Just because science isn't your best subject doesn't mean you shouldn't study for the upcoming test. And just because you're not into running doesn't mean you should walk the entire mile in phys ed.

Did you know that every opportunity comes from God? And He expects us to give our all in everything we do!

What are some things that you could do better with God's help?

....

....

....

....

....

....

....

....

....

....

....

....

....

....

....

You know that only one person gets a crown for being in a race even if many people run. You must run so you will win the crown.
1 CORINTHIANS 9:24

Temper Tantrums

Sometimes it's hard to keep your anger under control, especially when someone does something to hurt you. It's okay to throw a temper tantrum when you're super mad, right?

Wrong! Because you're a child of the King, God wants you to react the way He would react. Colossians 3:8 says that He wants you to put anger and hurtful words out of your life.

So, how do you do that? First, you need to pray about it. Tell God that you don't want to be mad anymore. Then, every time you start to get angry, take a deep breath. . .and trust that God will help your anger disappear!

What should you do when you're super mad?

....

....

....

....

....

....

....

....

....

....

....

....

....

....

....

....

....

....

Put out of your life these things also:
anger, bad temper, bad feelings toward
others, talk that hurts people, speaking
against God, and dirty talk.
COLOSSIANS 3:8

Women of God

Do you have good role models in your life?

God wants us to look for role models of everlasting value—these women are beautiful because of their deep love of God and their faith. Do you know any women whose lives show love, joy, peace, patience, kindness, goodness, faithfulness, gentleness, and self-control? If so, take time to thank these women for showing you—and others—what it means to be a woman of God.

Odds are, you're already a role model for someone younger than you. God wants you to show them the true beauty of Jesus in your heart too!

Make a list of the women who you look up to.

_A woman who fears the
Lord will be praised._
PROVERBS 31:30

The Biggest and Best Love

There are so many ways to show your love for others. You might exchange Valentine's Day cards with your best friend. You might help your mom cook dinner. You could pick a beautiful bouquet of flowers to brighten your grandma's day. While these are all wonderful ways to show your love, they don't come close to the perfect love God has for you.

Did you know that even when your heart was black with sin—when you were hard to love—God gave the greatest gift of love? He gave His perfect Son, Jesus, to die on the cross for our sins. What an amazing love!

Make a list of all the ways you can show your love for others this week.

....

....

....

....

....

....

....

....

....

....

....

....

....

....

....

....

....

This is love! It is not that we loved God but that He loved us. For God sent His Son to pay for our sins with His own blood.
1 JOHN 4:10

DRAW EVER NEARER TO THE HEAVENLY

CREATOR;

SEEK TO DO HIS WILL.

Heavenly Home

Home is probably one of your favorite places to be. Your room is exactly the way you like it. . .all your favorite things are exactly where you like them to be. But do you ever think about your *forever* home?

If you have accepted Jesus as your Savior, someday you'll get to live in heaven with Him forever.

Jesus tells us in John 14:2 that He has gone to heaven to prepare a place for us! He is getting our room ready in heaven.

Heaven is a perfect place—it's so perfect that you can't even begin to imagine how wonderful it is. Whenever you are having a rough day, remember this: Jesus is getting *your* room ready!

Write a paragraph describing what you think heaven will be like.

....
....
....
....
....
....
....
....
....
....
....
....
....
....
....
....
....
....
....

One thing I have asked from the Lord,
that I will look for: that I may live in the
house of the Lord all the days of my life,
to look upon the beauty of the Lord,
and to worship in His holy house.
PSALM 27:4

Perfect?

No one is perfect. . .except God. And because we're not perfect, we need Him in our lives in a very big way!

Does that mean you shouldn't try to do the right thing? Nope! You need to keep on trying! Do the best you can. But even when you mess up (and you will), run to God and tell Him you're sorry.

Imagine a lovely princess running into the throne room to visit her Father the King. That's what you do when you spend time praying! And in that place—that throne room—God forgives all your sins, then whispers, "I love you, daughter!"

Write a prayer in the space below thanking God for loving you just as you are.

....

....

....

....

....

....

....

....

....

....

....

....

....

....

For all [people] have sinned and have missed the shining-greatness of God. Anyone can be made right with God by the free gift of His loving-favor. It is Jesus Christ Who bought them with His blood and made them free from their sins.
ROMANS 3:23–24

Sticky Situations

Have you ever found yourself in a sticky situation? Maybe a friend wants you to do something wrong. What do you do? You don't want to risk making your friend mad, but you also want to do the right thing.

When you're tempted to do the wrong thing, God's Spirit will always nudge you and give you a little warning. That tiny voice of warning is your conscience. It stays with you no matter where you go or what you do.

It's always better to follow your conscience, even if it isn't easy. Your friend may be upset with you, but deep down inside, she'll know you did the right thing too.

In every situation, remember to always listen to your heart.

Have you ever been in a sticky situation? What did you do about it?

....

....

....

....

....

....

....

....

....

....

....

....

....

....

....

....

....

....

*I always try to live so my
own heart tells me I am not
guilty before God or man.*
ACTS 24:16

Mean Girls

You know her—the shy girl who sits in the back of the classroom. The girl who sits alone at lunchtime. The girl who gets picked on day in and day out.

Maybe there are days when you want to give her a hug and tell her that everything's going to be okay. . .that no one really likes those mean girls anyway. But something holds you back.

When you're having these feelings, say a little prayer asking God for help. He'll tell you what to do. And don't be surprised when you find yourself headed to the back of the classroom—with your arms open wide.

Have you ever been tempted to be a "mean girl" or have you ever been bullied? Write about it in the space below.

....

....

....

....

....

....

....

....

....

....

....

....

....

....

....

....

....

....

....

....

*Receive each other as Christ received
you. This will honor God.*
ROMANS 15:7

Show God

You like to know that you are loved, don't you? Of course you do! Everyone does. And it should come as no surprise that God wants to know that you love Him too.

The best way to show God that you love Him is to obey His commands. It isn't hard to do what God asks, because He is always there to help you do it. And the more you do the things He asks you to do, the happier you will be. You'll be well on your way to becoming the beautiful girl He created you to be!

How can you show God you love Him today?

....

....

....

....

....

....

....

....

....

....

....

....

....

....

....

....

....

....

....

....

Loving God means to obey His Word,
and His Word is not hard to obey.
1 JOHN 5:3

Copycat

It's annoying when girls imitate other girls, isn't it? But the truth is when another girl admires your behavior, your style, or your words so much that she'd like to mimic them, it's really a compliment.

Did you know that Jesus wants His children to imitate Him? He's given us perfect examples to follow by the life that He lived and through His teachings. And we show Him that we love Him when we try to be like Him.

How can you be more like Jesus? Spend time with Him; study His Word; get to know Him better; and learn what pleases Him. Once we truly know Him, we can we copy His example!

In what ways can you be more like Jesus?

....

....

....

....

....

....

....

....

....

....

....

....

....

....

....

....

....

....

....

Do as God would do.
Much-loved children want
to do as their fathers do.
EPHESIANS 5:1

All Grown-Up

Have you ever played "grown up," trying on your mom's shoes, dresses, and jewelry? Pretending you are an adult is fun, isn't it?

Sometimes we get so excited about what it's going to be like when we're older that we forget God created children for a reason. Don't ever look down on yourself because you're young. This breaks God's heart. Don't ever say, "But I'm just a kid! What can I do for God?" Because, the truth is, you can do plenty! And God wants you—no, He *needs* you—to understand that you don't have to wait till you're an adult to tell others about Him.

So, start now. Right where you are. Grab your tennies. . .and get running!

What can you do for God—right now?

....

....

....

....

....

....

....

....

....

....

....

....

....

....

....

....

....

But the Lord said to me, "Do not say,
'I am only a [child].' You must go
everywhere I send you. And you
must say whatever I tell you."
JEREMIAH 1:7

Jesus in Your Heart

When you ask Jesus to come into your heart, the Holy Spirit comes and makes His home inside of you, giving us hope for the future and helping us to know right from wrong.

Do you have the hope of knowing you will spend eternity with Jesus? If not, ask Him to come into your heart. Pray these words: "Dear Jesus, thank You for dying on the cross for my sins. Please forgive me for all the bad things I've done. Send the Holy Spirit to come and live in my heart so I can live in heaven forever with You someday. Amen."

If you prayed that prayer for the very first time, tell your parents or someone you trust from church. Ask them to help you get to know Jesus better!

How does life change when you invite Jesus into your heart?

....

....

....

....

....

....

....

....

....

....

....

....

....

....

....

....

....

Hope never makes us ashamed because the love of God has come into our hearts through the Holy Spirit Who was given to us.
ROMANS 5:5

God's Word

Do you make time for reading the Bible? A lot of people might tell you it's hard to understand God's Word, but it really isn't—not if you really want to "get it."

All you need to do is ask God to show you what He means, and He'll be glad to help you figure it out. And the more you read, the more you'll understand!

It's really important for you to spend time in God's Word, because there are lots of people who are teaching things that really aren't in the Bible. And if you know what's in the Bible, you'll know what's true and what isn't. Spend some time today with your Bible and the Author Himself!

Why is it important to spend time reading God's Word?

....

....

....

....

....

....

....

....

....

....

....

....

....

....

....

....

....

....

....

Do not let the many strange teachings
lead you in the wrong way. Our hearts
are made strong by God's loving-favor.
HEBREWS 13:9

"Everybody Does It"

Everybody lies. Everybody cheats. Or *do they*? And even if it's true, is it okay for *you* to do those things?

When you are a child of God, you are expected to *act* differently than the rest of the world. You don't do what everyone else is doing. You stand up for what's right. You are honest and obedient, even if it makes you unpopular.

God treasures His children. He blesses them for their obedience. He takes care of their needs and makes sure they have joy deep in their hearts. And best of all, He promises them a wonderful reward in heaven someday.

Don't be like "everybody." Be bold. Be different. Be a child of God.

In what ways do you act differently from everybody else?

Now then, if you will obey My voice
and keep My agreement, you will
belong to Me from among all nations.
EXODUS 19:5

A Little Kindness

It breaks God's heart when people don't get along. He wants His kids to love one another. But how is that possible, especially if people are mean?

The next time someone mistreats you, instead of getting mad, try a little kindness instead. The Bible says we should not return evil for evil. It doesn't help things to treat another person badly, after all. In fact, it just makes things worse!

This might sound crazy, but do something nice for the person who is treating you badly. Write her a nice note or give her a small gift. Then just watch and see if a little kindness doesn't go a long, long way in making things better!

How do you usually react when someone is mean to you? How *should* you react?

....

....

....

....

....

....

....

....

....

....

....

....

....

....

....

....

....

If the one who hates you is hungry, feed him. If he is thirsty, give him water.
PROVERBS 25:21

God's Plan

No matter what changes come your way, if you know Jesus, your life belongs to Him. Sometimes He allows change so that you will become stronger. And, sometimes, it's so that you will be able to help others who might go through something similar.

Things don't happen by accident or because God forgot to pay attention. He always knows what's happening in your life. And, more importantly, nothing can come into your life that doesn't first pass by Him. So don't struggle against His plan for you. You're God's special treasure. He knows what's best for you, and He'll take care of you, no matter what.

Have you ever had to deal with a hard change in your life? Share about it here.

....

....

....

....

....

....

....

....

....

....

....

....

....

....

....

....

....

....

This is the day that the Lord has made.
Let us be full of joy and be glad in it.
PSALM 118:24

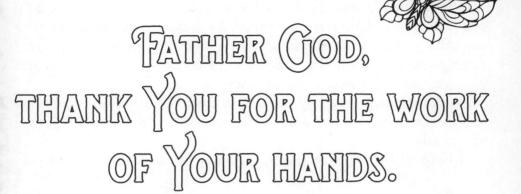

Father God,
thank You for the work of Your hands.

Honor Your Parents

The truth about parents is this: not even one of them is perfect. Parents are human—just like you. For the most part, they are trying to help you grow into a mature young woman. Even though you might not like everything your parents say or do, remember that God has a reason for putting you together in the same family. And He expects you to honor your parents—to respect and obey them.

When things go well, say "thanks" to God. When you are struggling, ask for His help. You just might be surprised to discover that it's *you* who needs to change.

Above all, honor your parents, and enjoy God's blessing that follows!

In what ways can you honor your parents?

....
....
....
....
....
....
....
....
....
....
....
....
....
....
....
....
....
....

*"Honor your father and your mother,
as the Lord your God has told you.
So your life may be long and it may
go well with you in the land the
Lord your God gives you."*
DEUTERONOMY 5:16

A Thankful Heart

Bad days? We all have them. . . .

While we can't always control things that go wrong, we *can* control our reaction to those things. So the next time you have a bad day, think about the wonderful things in your life—like your wonderful family, your cuddly pet, your bestie, your bedroom that's decorated just the way you like it... And you'll find yourself bouncing back fast from your crummy mood.

And last but not least, thank God for all the good stuff in your life. He'll be happy to hear from you!

Make a list of all the good things in your life.

....

....

....

....

....

....

....

....

....

....

....

....

....

....

....

....

....

....

....

....

....

....

Always give thanks for all things to God the Father in the name of our Lord Jesus Christ.
EPHESIANS 5:20

He Hears Me

Did you know that God *enjoys* hearing us ask Him for things that please Him?

Remember that God isn't a heavenly Santa Claus though. Our requests for new shoes and smartphones aren't the prayers He's wanting to hear. Instead, the prayers He's eagerly waiting on are the ones you pray for others who are hurting or in need.

Or if you need help making a decision, go ahead and ask God for guidance. And. . .even more important: have faith that He's already working out everything *before you even know* you have a need.

More than anything, God wants to hear from you. Talk to Him today, and then take time to listen for His voice.

Write a prayer in the space below.

....

....

....

....

....

....

....

....

....

....

....

....

....

....

....

....

....

*We are sure that if we ask anything
that He wants us to have, He will
hear us. If we are sure He hears us
when we ask, we can be sure He
will give us what we ask for.*
1 JOHN 5:14–15

Praise

Sometimes we get so distracted by the things of the world that we forget how great God is. But God doesn't want us to pay so much attention to those things that they become more important than He is.

God created the heavens and the earth. He made the world. He's the Ruler of the universe. And *you* are a princess in His Kingdom. How cool is that? God is the Great I AM.

How can you show Him He's more important to you than anything else? How about getting away from the screen for awhile and spending some time praising His name and being thankful that God loves you.

Give praise to your King! He loves hearing you cheer Him on!

What are some ways you can offer praise to God?

....

....

....

....

....

....

....

....

....

....

....

....

....

....

....

....

....

For great is the Lord. He is to be given much praise. And He is to be honored with fear more than all gods. For all the gods of the people are false gods. But the Lord made the heavens.

1 CHRONICLES 16:25–26

Forever with God

Have you ever felt cheated? Maybe you were overcharged for a purchase or you were skipped over when it was rightfully your turn to do something fun.

There are very few guarantees in life. But there is wonderful news about God's Kingdom! He guarantees a life with Him in heaven. . .forever! The moment we ask Jesus into our hearts and receive His gift of grace, we are given the keys to the Kingdom of heaven, and we become God's children forever and ever.

If you've received His gift, God is preparing a place for you in heaven right now! His plan for you to spend eternity with Him won't change—not ever. What are you doing to prepare for your guaranteed future with Him?

How does it feel to know you are God's child?

....

....

....

....

....

....

....

....

....

....

....

....

....

....

....

....

....

He gave the right and the power to become children of God to those who received Him. He gave this to those who put their trust in His name.
JOHN 1:12

Rain, Rain Go Away

Life is full of sad days. But even on your worst days, God is there. He has promised to never leave you alone. He cares when you have a rotten day. He sees your tears. He understands how you feel—even when no one else does. You are His precious child, and more than anything, He wants you to have the joy of Jesus in your heart!

Tell God what's troubling you today. No one loves you more than He does. And no one is better at calming the storms, chasing away the clouds, and letting the sunshine in.

Is there something hard you need to share with God today? Write your prayer in the space below.

....
....
....
....
....
....
....
....
....
....
....
....
....
....
....
....
....

Why are you sad, O my soul?
Why have you become troubled
within me? Hope in God, for I
will praise Him again for His
help of being near me.
Psalm 42:5

The Whole Puzzle

Our lives on earth are similar to a giant jigsaw puzzle (with no picture on the box to look at so we know what the completed puzzle should look like). We talk to God, asking for His help to make sense of the jumbled pieces we have on earth that we can't sort out. He is the only One who owns the finished picture. And He can see how the happiness and troubles in our lives will fit perfectly together in the end.

What trouble "pieces" do you have in your life? Ask God to take care of your problems by placing them in the right spot so they will ultimately work together for your good.

What "puzzle pieces" are giving you trouble in your life? Have you asked God to take care of them for you?

....

....

....

....

....

....

....

....

....

....

....

....

....

....

....

....

....

....

*We know that God makes all
things work together for the good
of those who love Him and are
chosen to be a part of His plan.*
ROMANS 8:28

Liar, Liar

You've heard the taunt, "Liar, liar, pants on fire." You may have even said it a time or two. Does it apply to you? Are you in the habit of telling lies—maybe not even big ones. . .but those little white lies that don't seem to make much of a difference?

The Bible is crystal clear on lying: God hates it! Even the little white lies that are meant to make others feel good. If you are really curious, look up Revelation 21:8. It describes what happens to people who make a lifelong habit of lying. *Yikes!* Ask God to help you be truthful in everything you say and do.

Have you ever told a little white lie? How did it make you feel?

....

....

....

....

....

....

....

....

....

....

....

....

....

....

....

....

....

The Lord hates lying
lips, but those who speak
the truth are His joy.
PROVERBS 12:22

Don't Give Up!

Have you ever tried something new—only to quickly get bored or give up?

God knows we have short attention spans. The great thing about God, though, is that when He starts something, He *always* sees it through.

God began His work in you the moment He thought you into existence. His project continued when you first heard about Him. He continued His work as you accepted Christ and became a Christian, and He'll continue working on you until you walk through the gates of heaven.

God doesn't get bored with you. He *never* will. Thank Him for His special attention to your life.

Have you ever wanted to give up on something? How did it turn out?

....

....

....

....

....

....

....

....

....

....

....

....

....

....

....

....

....

....

....

....

....

I am sure that God Who began the good work in you will keep on working in you until the day Jesus Christ comes again.
PHILIPPIANS 1:6

Pure Joy!

Think about some things you'd like to have. . . . Pretty easy, right? We always have a ready list of "stuff" that would make us just a little happier, don't we?

But have you ever made an A to Z, everything-that's-good-in-your-life list? From the simple to the big stuff—sunshine, your favorite food, your lovable (only occasionally annoying) sister or brother, your friends, your house, your favorite family vacation spot—you have too many blessings to name!

While we often tend to think about all of the things we don't have, the fact is every moment of the day, no matter where you look, you can find at least one item to thank God for—one blessing in your life. Now that's reason to celebrate. . .all day long!

What are some simple blessings in your life?

....

....

....

....

....

....

....

....

....

....

....

....

....

....

....

....

....

....

....

....

Be full of joy always because
you belong to the Lord.
Again I say, be full of joy!
PHILIPPIANS 4:4

Stuck Up?

Girls—even Christian girls—sometimes act a little, well. . .stuck up. They think they're better than the others in their group. Maybe you've met girls like that. Maybe you've been a girl like that.

The problem with thinking you're better than others is that the Bible teaches us to do exactly the opposite—to think of others as better than ourselves. *It's true!* And if we're only focused on ourselves (our clothes, hair, popularity and so forth), we're not really thinking of others, are we?

Today's verse is a great reminder that we shouldn't put others down to make ourselves look better. Nope! God wants us to put others first. And to do that, we just have to lay aside our selfishness and love others the way He loves them—*and us too!*

Why is it sometimes hard to put others first?

....

....

....

....

....

....

....

....

....

....

....

....

....

....

....

....

....

....

....

....

Nothing should be done because of pride or thinking about yourself. Think of other people as more important than yourself.
PHILIPPIANS 2:3

That Lovely Face!

God made you. . .you! And He did it on purpose!

Think about it—the King of kings decided even before you were born just what you would look like. He selected the color of your hair, your skin, your eyes—*everything*! He decided how tall or short you would be, how thin, how chubby. . .and dropped in some extra-special talents and abilities, just for fun! Your awesome Creator took great care in making all of these very important decisions.

When God looks at you, He loves what He sees! So the next time you look in the mirror and want to grumble, take the time to thank Him for making you. . .*you*!

How does it feel knowing God took great care in making you?

....
....
....
....
....
....
....
....
....
....
....
....
....
....
....
....
....
....

"Before I started to put you together in your mother, I knew you. Before you were born, I set you apart as holy. I chose you to speak to the nations for Me."
JEREMIAH 1:5

You CAN!

Legends tell of heroes sent on spectacular quests—to slay the fire-breathing dragon, find the lost ring, or rescue the princess from a tower. All of these things seemed impossible. But with a little luck and some unexpected help, the hero managed to do it.

What's your impossible quest? Whatever it is, have courage! You have a powerful Helper on your side! And God has an unlimited supply of courage designed to defeat nervous jitters. He knows the answer to every question. With Him by your side, you can do *anything*! As long as you have done your best by practicing, studying, and working hard, God is happy to help.

Be bold! God is right there with you, helping you fulfill your quest.

What can you do with God's help?

_____

_____

_____

_____

_____

_____

_____

_____

_____

_____

_____

_____

_____

_____

_____

_____

_____

_____

_____

*I can do all things because
Christ gives me the strength.*
PHILIPPIANS 4:13

Shine Your Light

Have you ever enjoyed the embarrassment or humiliation of someone you dislike?

If so, it's important to know that Jesus is sad when we find satisfaction in the hurts and embarrassments of others. (And after all, you *do* know better, don't you?)

As Christians, we're to love others—that means *all* people, *including* our enemies. And, although it's a hard thing to do, that means reaching out and supporting them in Christian love rather than taking delight in their hardships. Say a prayer for your enemies today, and ask God to help you shine your light for Him.

Have you said a prayer for your enemies lately? Write one in the space below.

....

....

....

....

....

....

....

....

....

....

....

....

....

....

....

....

....

....

....

Do not be full of joy when the one who hates you falls. Do not let your heart be glad when he trips.
Proverbs 24:17

Spending Time

Are you the kind of student who dives right into her homework when she gets home from school? Are you the kind of girl who sets right to the task when it's time to clean your room, resisting the urge to read all of those texts from a friend?

What about spending time with God? That should also be part of our daily routine. And God wants you to do your best in your work—school and chores.

Talk to God today and ask for His help in spending your time wisely. That would be a *great* use of time!

What is your favorite way to spend time with God?

_[A person] who obeys the king's law
will have no trouble, for a wise heart
knows the right time and way._
ECCLESIASTES 8:5

Smile!

Do you love to dress up?

The truth is, fancy clothes and matching accessories aren't necessary to make a girl truly beautiful. In fact, the most important thing you can wear was given to you by God Himself. Can you guess what it is? Your *smile*!

Smiling is a reflection of the beauty *inside* you. It's hard to frown when you're bubbling over with joy.

So. . .SMILE! Use your God-given beauty accessory to welcome the new girl, comfort a gloomy friend, and share your happiness—all without saying a single word. You won't have to. Your smile says it all!

What is true beauty?

A glad heart makes a happy face, but when he heart is sad, the spirit is broken.
PROVERBS 15:13

Never Lonely

We all have lonely moments from time to time—moments when we feel like no one cares, no one wants to listen to our problems, no one wants to spend time with us. . . And in those moments, we can choose to be sad and miserable, or we can choose to find comfort in the One who will never leave us lonely.

Our heavenly Father promises that He'll always be here for us, even when our friends and family let us down. When there's no one for us to turn to, we can always talk to God. He'll listen; He'll comfort; He'll encourage. He's always there—24/7. And He's waiting to hear from you now!

Whenever you feel lonely, do you remember that God is *always* there? How does it feel to know you're *never* alone?

....

....

....

....

....

....

....

....

....

....

....

....

....

....

....

....

....

....

....

....

....

"I am with you always,
even to the end of the world."
MATTHEW 28:20

A Life That Is Pleasing

As a Christian girl, you will have lots of people watching every move you make as you grow up. People are watching to see if you are really living out what you believe.

If you are truly living out your faith every day—and others can see a difference in you—you just might find some of your observers checking out this "Christian thing" for themselves. So make sure you are living a life that is pleasing to the Lord. Get rid of anything that might be in the way of your relationship with Him, and ask Him to help you live out your faith each day.

Does your faith make a difference in how you behave?

....

....

....

....

....

....

....

....

....

....

....

....

....

....

....

....

....

....

Let us put every thing out of our lives that keeps us from doing what we should. Let us keep running in the race that God has planned for us.
HEBREWS 12:1

The Best Gift

Chances are your parents are already proud of you—because you're their daughter! You don't have to go out of your way to knock their socks off. In fact, there's only one thing that your parents expect from you. . . *obedience*.

Nothing thrills your parents more than when you follow their rules without arguing and complaining. And that is worth more than any gift you could give them. Not only does it make your parents happy, it pleases your heavenly Father as well.

Whether or not you agree with their rules, whether or not you understand their wishes. . .obey. Why? Because it's the *right* thing to do!

Why should you obey your parents—even when you don't completely understand their rules?

....

....

....

....

....

....

....

....

....

....

....

....

....

....

....

....

....

....

....

Children, as Christians,
obey your parents.
This is the right thing to do.
EPHESIANS 6:1

What If?

Everyone struggles with the fear of failure at one time or another. But God doesn't want us to give up on something before we even get started. That's why He encourages us to talk to Him about our worries and then leave the details to Him. He'll support you in whatever you seek out to accomplish.

Today ask God to erase those nerve-wracking "what-ifs" from your mind and believe that He will provide just the right amount of courage and strength that you need. With God on your side, you'll be amazed at what you can do. That's a promise!

What are your most bothersome worries? Have you asked God to help erase them from your mind?

....

....

....

....

....

....

....

....

....

....

....

....

....

....

....

....

....

"Peace I leave with you. My peace I give to you. I do not give peace to you as the world gives. Do not let your hearts be troubled or afraid."
JOHN 14:27

Be Bold!

Some talents seem to be inclined to bring honor to God. Singers join the church choir, and musicians play on the praise team. Natural teachers lead a Sunday school class, and public speakers prepare devotions for youth group.

But the truth is that *every gift* from God can be used for His glory. Soccer players can share Jesus with non-Christians on the field. Poets can write God's encouragement to people who need it. Good listeners help others get through difficult times.

Whatever your talents are, share them with others. If you don't know what your gifts are, ask God to show them to you. Your heavenly Father is proud of everything you accomplish for His glory.

What are some of your talents? How can you use them for God's glory?

....

....

....

....

....

....

....

....

....

....

....

....

....

....

....

....

....

....

....

....

*In a big house there are not only
things made of gold and silver,
but also of wood and clay. . . .
Some are used every day.*
2 TIMOTHY 2:20

Peacemaker

Getting along with others isn't always easy—especially if someone is determined to have her own way. But treating that person the way she is treating you will only add fuel to the fire. Making peace means going out of *your* way to get along. Try letting your pesky brother have the last cookie or volunteering to do the dishes when it's his turn. Say something nice to that hard-to-deal-with schoolmate. Be a friend to the unfriendly.

A little extra kindness may be all it takes to end the feud between you and your brother or sister. And that annoying schoolmate might turn out to be a great friend. Best of all, you'll earn the reputation—on earth and in heaven—as a peacemaker.

In what ways can you be a peacemaker?

_____

_____

_____

_____

_____

_____

_____

_____

_____

_____

_____

_____

_____

_____

_____

_____

Those who make peace are happy, because they will be called the [children] of God.
MATTHEW 5:9

Listen Up!

To *really* listen means you're focused on what's being said to you. You're not planning your next hang-out with friends. You're not watching your favorite Netflix show or sending a text message to your BFF. When you're really listening, you hear *everything* the other person says. *Every single word.*

You have so much to learn from the adults in your life. When your parents ask for your attention, it's because they're trying to teach you something. The best way you can show them you're learning is to do what they say. In other words. . .to listen means to obey. So listen up!

How can you show others that you're *really* listening?

....

....

....

....

....

....

....

....

....

....

....

....

....

....

....

....

Hear your father's teaching. . .
and do not turn away from your
mother's teaching. For they are
a glory to your head and a chain
of beauty around your neck.
PROVERBS 1:8–9

Loving Others

God has given us a commandment to love each other as He has loved us. But what about the people who don't seem to be very likeable at all? How can you learn to love them?

Well, as God's daughter, you know about what God has done for you and how much He loves you. You know He sent His Son to die on a cross for you so that you can have a home in heaven with Him one day. And you know He didn't do it just for you—it was also for all those people who don't seem very lovable.

If you're having a hard time loving someone, ask God for help. Ask Him to let His love shine through you to someone else. When you do, you'll be proving to the world that you are God's child.

How can you love others better?

....

....

....

....

....

....

....

....

....

....

....

....

....

....

....

....

....

....

"I give you a new Law. You are to love each other. You must love each other as I have loved you. If you love each other, all men will know you are My followers."
JOHN 13:34–35

It's Just Stuff

Could you live without Netflix? What about the internet? Cell phone? Video games? What would you do if all of those things disappeared—never to return?

Girls today have lots and lots of "stuff," but some of it keeps us from doing what we should be doing. Imagine you're watching YouTube videos. The hours go by, and you don't even realize it. Before long, the whole afternoon has passed. You've missed out on time with your family or reading your Bible. You haven't done your homework, and you forgot to text your grandma back.

See how our "stuff" gets in the way? Here's a fun challenge: for one full day, give it up! Don't think you can do it? Give it a try! After all. . .it's just stuff!

How would you feel if you woke up tomorrow and all your stuff was gone?

....

....

....

....

....

....

....

....

....

....

....

....

....

....

....

....

....

....

....

....

....

Do not love the world or anything in the world. If anyone loves the world, the Father's love is not in him.
1 JOHN 2:15

Busy, Busy

You are a busy girl! Being busy and having a lot of fun activities to do is fun. But you know what? The devil likes to make us so busy that we forget to spend time with God.

All of our activities are fine and good as long as we are keeping God first in our life and not cramming so much into our schedule that we never have time to go to church or pray or read our Bibles. Feel like you don't have any control over your busy schedule? Talk to your parents and ask them to help you with your priorities. Make a list of what you *have* to do and what you *want* to do. Pray and ask the Lord to help you decide what is most important. Remember who is in control and let God be your "Day Planner."

Do you feel like you have control over your schedule? Are there some unimportant things you need to remove from your to-do list?

....

....

....

....

....

....

....

....

....

....

....

....

....

....

....

....

....

....

*There are many plans in a
[person's] heart, but it is the
Lord's plan that will stand.*
PROVERBS 19:21

Take a Look Inside

Did you know that there are a lot of people in our country who haven't heard about God's love?

Each of us should be ready to share our faith with others, but we should also be living each day so that they can see Jesus in us. If we are dishonest, or use bad language, or cheat, do you think they'll want to know the same Jesus we claim to love? Will they see any difference in us than in their friends who aren't Christians?

Take a look inside yourself. . . . Are there any changes you need to make in your behavior so you can be a better witness for Him?

When others look at your life, do they see Jesus? Why or why not?

....

....

....

....

....

....

....

....

....

....

....

....

....

....

....

....

....

....

....

*You are to tell all
[people] what you
have seen and heard.*
ACTS 22:15

Valuable

Some fans research the biography of their favorite celebrities, memorizing facts about their childhood and family. Although it may seem silly to someone on the outside, to a fan, even the most boring fact seems important.

Did you know that God's love for and interest in you runs even deeper than an obsessed fan? He cares so much for you that He knows *every* fact about you that nobody—*even you*—knows, like how many hairs are on your head at this very moment. He knows every thought you think, every emotion you feel, every action you take.

If God cares to know you so intimately, just think about how valuable you are to Him!

How well do you think God knows you?

....

....

....

....

....

....

....

....

....

....

....

....

....

....

....

....

....

"Are not five small birds sold
for two small pieces of money?
God does not forget even one of
the birds. God knows how many
hairs you have on your head.
Do not be afraid. You are worth
more than many small birds."
LUKE 12:6–7

True Happiness

Do you know somebody at church or school who seems to get everything they want? Do you ever find yourself wishing that you were that person?

Many people spend their whole life trying to make more money so that they can have everything they want. They think that the more "stuff" they have, the happier they will be. The Bible teaches us that it is not worth it to live that kind of life. You end up chasing after earthly pleasures that can never bring you true happiness. Instead, we should be chasing after God and His will for our lives. Only then can we know true happiness here on this earth and in heaven as well. Give it a try!

Why is chasing after God so important?

....

....

....

....

....

....

....

....

....

....

....

....

....

....

....

....

....

....

....

....

*For what does a man have if he gets
all the world and loses his own soul?*
MARK 8:36

The Great Pretender

Remember Superman? The superhero with X-ray vision, the one who could see through anything? Well, we have someone even more super than that! He's God!

God can see through anything. He knows what you do and what is in your heart all the time. He knows if you are pretending to care about someone but, in reality, don't even like them. He knows when you don't always stand up for what's right. Neither scenario is part of His plan for you.

So, what's a girl to do? Turn to Him and ask for some of His superpower. He'll help you learn to love others when you think you can't. He'll give you the strength to stand up for what's right. He'll help you to do these things without pretending—*really*.

Do you ever find yourself pretending—rather than being the real you?

....
....
....
....
....
....
....
....
....
....
....
....
....
....
....
....
....
....
....

Be sure your love is true love.
Hate what is sinful. Hold on
to whatever is good.
ROMANS 12:9

Your Special Story

Maybe you've been asked about your faith before. Did you know what to say? God tells His followers to be prepared to answer anyone who asks us why we believe what we believe.

When someone opens the door for you to share your testimony, talk about your faith in three minutes. . .

Minute one: Talk about what your life was like and what struggles you had before you accepted Christ.

Minute two: Share your story of how you became a Christian and what steps you took to come to that point.

Minute three: Tell about how your life has changed since beginning a relationship with Jesus and the hope you have in spending eternity with Him in heaven.

Your testimony is a special story that is unique to you. It's an amazing recollection of a miracle God performed in you, His child!

What is your unique story?

....

....

....

....

....

....

....

....

....

....

....

....

....

....

....

*Your heart should be holy and set apart
for the Lord God. Always be ready to
tell everyone who asks you why you
believe as you do. Be gentle as
you speak and show respect.*
1 PETER 3:15

The Green-Eyed Monster

Lurking behind the next corner, a creature is watching, waiting to grab his next victim. His name is Envy, and his purpose is to spread misery and gloom to as many people as possible.

"It's not fair!" he'll whisper. "Why does *she* have all of the talent? Why can't you be as pretty as *she is?*" Before you know it, you'll be ensnared in his trap. And all the while, you'll become more and more miserable. Envy wants you to forget who you really are—a child of the heavenly King.

Tell Envy to scram. You don't need other people's looks or talents or brains. You're terrific just the way you are. . .the way God created you.

Have you ever been attacked by "the green-eyed monster"? Share about it here.

....

....

....

....

....

....

....

....

....

....

....

....

....

....

....

....

....

....

Let us not become proud in
ways in which we should not.
We must not make hard feelings
among ourselves as Christians
or make anyone jealous.
GALATIANS 5:26

Scripture Memorization

God's Word is a lamp that will shine light onto your path as you walk through life. Its guidance will help you avoid a painful walk through the dark.

Make it a priority to memorize God's Word. Being able to remember a scriptural truth and to know the words of God helps dark things become very clear. The verses you learn will help you when temptation comes your way. They will comfort you through troubled times. They will remind you of how you can please God in your daily life. They are like a light in a dark place. Let God's Word light the way for you in the darkness of the world. Let it shine!

What is your favorite Bible verse and why?

*Your Word is a lamp
to my feet and a
light to my path.*
PSALM 119:105

Your Beautiful Heart

Have you ever stood in front of the mirror for hours, wishing those freckles would disappear or trying to straighten all those curls? Do you let your appearance change your attitude?

God's Word tells us in 1 Samuel 16:7 that God looks only at our hearts. You are beautiful just the way God made you, but what really matters is the condition of your heart. It's hard to imagine when you are right in the middle of it, but ten years from now no one will care (or even remember!) if you had to wear glasses in school. Ask God to help you worry less about what you look like on the outside and more about what your heart looks like on the inside.

When you look at others, do you look at their hearts—or do you focus on outside appearances?

....

....

....

....

....

....

....

....

....

....

....

....

....

....

....

....

*"Which of you can make yourself
a little taller by worrying? If you
cannot do that which is so little,
why do you worry about
other things?"*
LUKE 12:25–26

Forget about It!

When a friend hurts your feelings, you will probably be angry—and maybe even a little sad. You might even hold on to your hurt feelings for a while. After all, friends aren't supposed to hurt each other, are they?

No doubt about it, forgiving your friend will be hard. But this could be the perfect opportunity to reflect God's amazing love into the life of someone else—a way for your friend to see God through your actions. After all, God's Word gives us this bit of wisdom: "My children, let us not love with words or in talk only. Let us love by what we do and in truth" (1 John 3:18).

Talk to God and ask Him to take away your hurt feelings, and then ask Him for His help in extending forgiveness to your friend. And after you forgive her, forget about it. God will be delighted!

When was the last time you forgave someone who hurt your feelings?

....

....

....

....

....

....

....

....

....

....

....

....

....

....

....

....

....

It is to his honor to forgive and forget a wrong done to [you].
PROVERBS 19:11

A Lump of Clay

What do you want to be when you grow up? A lawyer? A teacher? A missionary? All of these occupations are important.

It's easy to come up with our own plan for our life, but God is the Potter—we are just the clay. The clay doesn't do anything on its own to become a vase or a pot. It just lies on the wheel, waiting for the potter to form it into a very special creation.

Your Potter wants to mold you into a unique creation as well. But in order for you to become a lovely work of art, you need to allow Him to do His work in you. Be willing to do what He wants you to do and go where He wants you to go. Only then will you truly be joyful.

What are your future plans? Do they match up with God's plan for your life?

....

....

....

....

....

....

....

....

....

....

....

....

....

....

....

....

....

But the pot he was making of clay did not come out like he wanted it. So the pot-maker used the clay to make another pot that pleased him.
JEREMIAH 18:4

Grumbling vs. Praising

People who complain a lot aren't very fun to be around. As Christians, we shouldn't be complainers. In all situations, we should think more about the things that went right and the blessings we received.

When you're tempted to grumble about something, stop and ask God to help you find a good thing in that situation. Ask Him to show you what good can come from it and to help you learn from each thing that happened.

As followers of Christ, we know that everything comes through the hand of God. So, when talking to others, rather than blaming God for the bad things, you should focus on the good things, giving God the glory.

What are some things you grumble about? What can you do to stop?

....

....

....

....

....

....

....

....

....

....

....

....

....

....

....

....

....

*I will honor the Lord at
all times. His praise will
always be in my mouth.*
PSALM 34:1

Get Rid of It!

Have you ever tried hiding your faults? Disguising the ugly parts of your personality so no one can see them?

Maybe you're a procrastinator, always putting things off until the last minute. Perhaps you have the bad habit of rolling your eyes or sighing when you're told to do something. These things are faults—areas in your life that need to be cleaned up—just like your bedroom. And rather than trying to hide them in hopes that they won't easily be seen, God expects us to get rid of them.

Throw out the junk in your life. Strive every day to overcome your faults. Confess them to others and ask for their help in getting rid of your bad qualities. Cleaning up your "spiritual room" is a lot of work, but when you're done, you'll earn a great big thumbs-up from God.

Are you hiding any "junk" in your life? If so, what should you do with it?

....

....

....

....

....

....

....

....

....

....

....

....

....

....

....

....

....

....

....

....

....

Who can see his own mistakes?
Forgive my sins that I do not see.
PSALM 19:12

Be a Barnabas!

Barnabas was a man from the Bible who was a friend of Paul. You can read more about him in the book of Acts. He was known for encouraging other people.

It is so important to be an encourager. . .and there are a lot of people in need of some encouragement! Can you think of some? What can you do to help?

When people think of you, do they think of you as an encourager, or do they think of you as a girl who is down all the time or only thinks about herself? Which would you rather be—one who lifts others up or one who brings others down? Ask God to help you think more about others and to be a better encourager—with all your heart.

What are some ways you can be a Barnabas today?

....

....

....

....

....

....

....

....

....

....

....

....

....

....

....

....

....

....

When he got there and saw how good God had been to them, he was full of joy. He told them to be true and faithful to the Lord.
ACTS 11:23

Lift 'Em Up!

What if you told your best friend (or maybe one of your parents) that you were going through something hard and asked them to pray for you? Wouldn't that make you feel better? It feels so good to know someone is lifting up your name in prayer. And that works the other way around too. If you tell someone you're going to be praying for them, they're counting on you to really do it.

But how do you know who to pray for? Try this: put together a list. Include your family members and add friends who are going through struggles. Also add people from your church.) Then every day, sit down with your list and pray over every name. Lift 'em up, girl!

Who is on your prayer list for today?

....

....

....

....

....

....

....

....

....

....

....

....

....

....

....

....

....

....

....

*I always thank God
when I speak of you
in my prayers.*
PHILEMON 1:4

Secret Keeper?

How many times have you been told, "I have something to tell you, but you *can't* tell *anyone!*" Often that begins a discussion about gossip or some other top-secret information. But what if a friend confessed, "I'm taking drugs"? Is that a secret you should keep?

When a friend is harming herself or being harmed, she needs help. Tell her that you'd like to go with her so that she can get the help she needs. She may feel comfortable with a pastor, a teacher, or even your parent.

God gave us friends to not only have fun with but also to help when things get tough. Just as you need help from others at times, they need help from you. And with strength from God, you can be part of the plan in getting your friend the help she needs.

What secrets are okay to keep? Which ones should you share with a trusted adult?

....

....

....

....

....

....

....

....

....

....

....

....

....

....

....

....

....

....

"Kindness from a friend should be shown to a man without hope, or he might turn away from the fear of the All-powerful."
JOB 6:14

Wildfire

Have you ever heard news about someone else that you just couldn't keep to yourself? God calls this sharing of news gossip. And he *hates* it because it devastates relationships, ruins reputations, and shatters self-confidence. Gossip is the spark that can ignite an angry fire among friends, and once it starts, it's hard to stop.

So what should you do if you're stuck in a line of gossipers? Smother the flames by changing the subject. If that doesn't work, explain that you'd rather not hear about the news and that the person being talked about probably doesn't want everyone to know.

Ask God to make you aware of the gossip fires in your life so that you can work toward extinguishing them.

How can you stop gossip in its tracks?

_____

_____

_____

_____

_____

_____

_____

_____

_____

_____

_____

_____

_____

_____

*When there is no wood, the fire
goes out. Where there is no
one telling secret stories about
people, arguing stops.*
PROVERBS 26:20

Forgiven

Have you ever messed up big-time and thought, *Uh-oh, now I've done it. I feel so bad about what I've done. I wonder if God will ever forgive me?*

While all of us will occasionally make mistakes and fail to be "perfect," it's a comfort to know that God has promised in His Word to forgive us—*no matter what.* He loves each of us so much that our mistakes won't cause Him to turn His back on us—no matter how big or bad our sin may seem.

Need forgiveness from God? Just ask, and you'll have it!

How does it feel knowing God will forgive you—no matter what?

....

....

....

....

....

....

....

....

....

....

....

....

....

....

....

....

....

....

"Come now, let us think about this together," says the Lord. "Even though your sins are bright red, they will be as white as snow. Even though they are dark red, they will be like wool."

ISAIAH 1:18

Break Away!

Whether you're with your friends, your family, or the people from your church. . .life can get really loud and crazy! It's exciting to hang out with lots of people and have a great time, but it's also wonderful to sneak away for some quiet time with your heavenly Father. He doesn't just want you to talk to Him; He wants you to listen for His voice. And it's easier to hear His voice when you're quiet and still, which is why it's important to get away from the crowd.

In the secret place, you're telling God that you love hanging out with Him. Every girl should tell her Creator that she adores Him. So break away from the crowd today—and do just that!

Where is your favorite place to spend time with God and why?

....
....
....
....
....
....
....
....
....
....
....
....
....
....
....
....
....
....

*Then He went away by Himself
to pray in a desert.*
LUKE 5:16

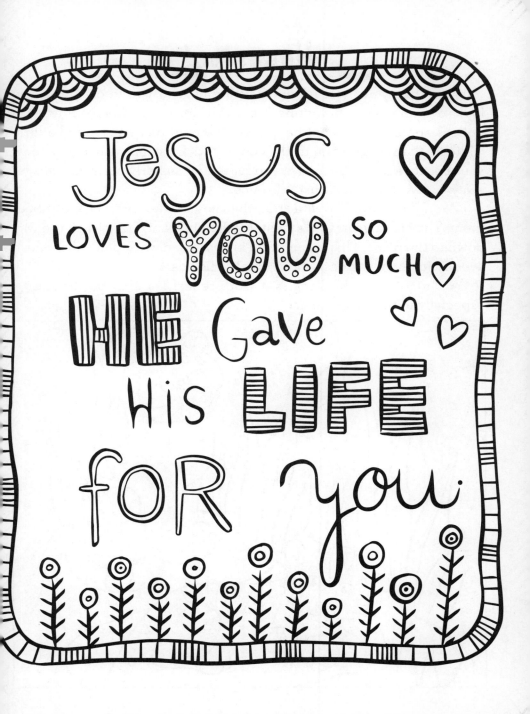

Honestly!

Imagine this—your best friend is sitting next to you in class and she looks over at your test, wanting to copy the answers. Then your teacher notices and asks you what happened. It would be easier to tell a little white lie than confess the truth, wouldn't it? Especially since you know your best friend will be mad at you for telling on her! Surely you can get away with a "little" lie. . .just this once.

Wrong! The problem with little white lies is there's nothing little about them! They're huge in God's sight. More important, He sees all the way down to the heart. That means God knows when we're being dishonest, even if no one else does—and it breaks His heart.

A daughter of the King is a truth-teller! Dare to be different—especially in the tough times!

Why is it sometimes hard to tell the truth?

....
....
....
....
....
....
....
....
....
....
....
....
....
....
....
....
....
....
....

Lips that tell the truth will last forever, but a lying tongue lasts only for a little while.
PROVERBS 12:19

What about Me?

Is doing good really worth all the effort? Especially when no one notices or recognizes your hard work?

The truth is if we focus on others instead of ourselves, we'll begin to see the effect of our good deeds. And God will have a hand in that. He sees what we're doing to make a difference in the lives of others; and He promises that we will experience something good because of it. While people may overlook or forget our kindnesses, isn't it wonderful to know that God never will?

Today, ask the Lord to give you the strength and energy you need to keep up the good work. And then wait and see what good things He brings your way!

Is "doing good" worth all the effort? Why or why not?

Do not let yourselves get tired of doing good. If we do not give up, we will get what is coming to us at the right time.
GALATIANS 6:9

Step It Up!

God loves it when you "step it up" and give Him your very best.

If you're looking for some great ways to do that, here are some suggestions: Give God your very best attitude (even when it's really hard)! Give Him your best time of day. (Don't wait until you're too tired to pray and read your Bible.) Give an offering at church. (Putting money in the offering plate is a great way to show that you're dedicated to Him.)

There are a zillion ways to do more for God! And a daughter of the King loves to give—of her time, talents, and treasures. She gives her Father her very best. . .so step it up!

What are some ways you plan to "step it up"?

....

....

....

....

....

....

....

....

....

....

....

....

....

....

....

....

*Do your best to know that God is
pleased with you. Be as a workman who
has nothing to be ashamed of. Teach
the words of truth in the right way.*
2 TIMOTHY 2:15

How Big Is God?

Remember the story of David and Goliath? A shepherd boy named David faced a huge giant named Goliath who was a Philistine. David had courage because he remembered that God was bigger than anything and anyone, and that He was always with him.

David said "The Lord Who saved me from the foot of the lion and from the foot of the bear, will save me from the hand of this Philistine." (1 Samuel 17:37). David defeated the giant with only a stone and a sling because the power of God was with him.

Do you know that God's power is with you too? Is there something in your life right now that just seems way too big to handle by yourself? Remember that God is bigger, and just like He was with David, He will be with you too!

Is there a "Goliath" in your life? If there is, what do you plan on doing about it?

....

....

....

....

....

....

....

....

....

....

....

....

....

....

....

....

....

....

What can we say about all these things? Since God is for us, who can be against us?
ROMANS 8:31

Words, Words, Words

Bullies tear others down to make themselves feel better. They're mean and rude and no fun to be around.

God hates bullying—even in small doses. Mean words can leave lasting wounds. They can damage people's self-esteem and even cause them to be mean to other people.

God's will for His children is that every word that comes out of our mouths is helpful and builds others up. That doesn't mean we have to be fake about our words. God wants sincere encouragement to be on our lips. Ask God to give you a spirit of goodness that spills over into your daily conversation. You never know when a kind word will brighten someone else's day.

What are some encouraging words you can share with others today?

....

....

....

....

....

....

....

....

....

....

....

....

....

....

....

....

*Watch your talk! No bad words should
be coming from your mouth. Say what
is good. Your words should help
others grow as Christians.*
EPHESIANS 4:29

Healthy

What are you feeding your soul? Are you filling your heart and mind with the world's music, movies, and TV programs? If so, retrain your appetite by spending more time reading God's Word, listening to Christian music, and reading good books.

You may not always feel like obeying God's Word, attending church, or taking part in wholesome activities, but doing those things over and over helps to develop your appetite for them. Jesus tells us that if we come to Him, He will fill us with spiritual food so that we will never be hungry. So, even though you may not always feel like learning more about God or doing the things you know you should, do them anyway. He will bless you for your faithfulness, and you may be surprised at how your appetite changes.

What are you "feeding" your soul?

....

....

....

....

....

....

....

....

....

....

....

....

....

....

....

....

Jesus said to them, "I am the
Bread of Life. He who comes
to Me will never be hungry.
He who puts his trust in
Me will never be thirsty."
JOHN 6:35

Sugar and Spice

People sometimes have mixed-up motives. You will probably even be wrongly accused of something now and then.

Thankfully, we are not accountable to other people for our actions. We are only accountable to God, who sees what is done and understands the motives of the heart. So, no matter what people say about your actions, if your intentions are pure and you are doing right before God, you have nothing to worry about. Jesus was wrongly accused, but He knew that His Father knew the truth, so He didn't even try to defend Himself. Try to live with such confidence that it just doesn't matter what other people say; it only matter what Jesus says.

Why does it matter that you are only accountable to God for your actions?

....
....
....
....
....
....
....
....
....
....
....
....
....
....
....
....

When you are around people who do not know God, be careful how you act. Even if they talk against you as wrong-doers, in the end they will give thanks to God for your good works when Christ comes again.
1 PETER 2:12

Let Your Worries Fly

Imagine you're holding something in your hand. You don't want to let go, no matter how many times you're told you should. So you keep it clutched in your fist.

What's inside? What have you been holding onto?

Worries? Well, it's time to let them go. Give them to God! His hands are much bigger than yours, after all—and He wants to hold them for you.

Wave your hands up in the air. Feel those burdens lifting? Can you see your worries flying away? You were never meant to hold on to them in the first place, you know. God wants His daughters to live a worry-free life. So the next time you're tempted to worry, remember to open up those hands. . .and let your troubles fly far, far away—straight to the heart of your Father.

Is it easy to give your worries to God? Why or why not?

....

....

....

....

....

....

....

....

....

....

....

....

....

....

....

....

....

....

....

Give all your worries to Him
because He cares for you.
1 PETER 5:7

New Life

You know that when you asked Jesus to be your Savior, you received new life, but have you ever really stopped to think about what that means?

Think about nature in springtime. You see a nest full of eggs. It doesn't look like much, but you know that inside those eggs new little creatures are waiting to hatch and begin life. When they finally do hatch, they're still helpless and awkward, but oh, the potential that's there! When you trusted Jesus, you were like that little bird—a new creature. You had a ways to go in your spiritual walk, but with Jesus you could realize the full potential of your new life.

Have you stopped and said thank you to Jesus for giving you a new life? If not, write a prayer of thanks in the space below.

....

....

....

....

....

....

....

....

....

....

....

....

....

....

....

....

....

....

....

....

Christ lives in me.
GALATIANS 2:20

Happiness That Lasts!

Your friend just got a new iPhone, and you can't help but feel a little envious. After all, you've been wanting a new smartphone for as long as you can remember. . .and you're *still* waiting. The more you hear about your friend's new "treasure," the harder it is for you to be even a little happy for her.

It's so easy to fall into the I-want trap. But once you get that longed-for item, will you really be satisfied? Maybe for just a little while, but eventually you will have an itch for something new.

In God's Word, He reminds us that earthly things won't ever make us truly happy. Only when we focus on things eternal—like our relationship with Jesus Christ—will we find happiness that lasts for a lifetime.

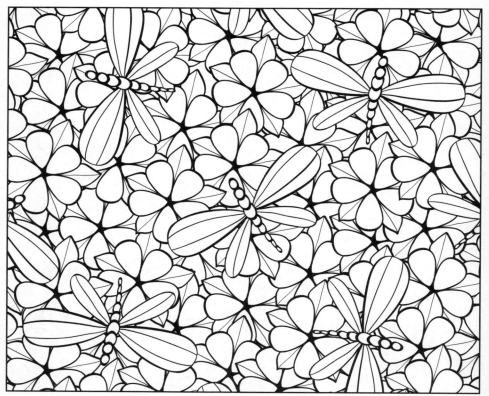

What makes you truly happy?

....

....

....

....

....

....

....

....

....

....

....

....

....

....

....

"Watch yourselves! Keep from wanting all kinds of things you should not have. A man's life isnot made up of things, even if he has many riches."
LUKE 12:15

God-Confidence

Philippians 4:13 tells us that we can do all things through Christ who gives us strength. So if you're one of those girls who's short on confidence, ask God to give you His confidence. You can do all things through Christ!

So the next time you have to get up in class and read a report or do anything else that brings you center stage, remember that although self-confidence is useless, God-confidence is all-strengthening and just a prayer away!

If you happen to be one of those girls with a ton of self-confidence, ask God to help you focus more on Him. That way whenever you do something in public, the focus will be on God instead of on you. God-confidence is so much better!

Do you have God-confidence? How do you know?

So watch yourself! The person who thinks he can stand against sin had better watch that he does not fall into sin.

1 CORINTHIANS 10:12

From Invisible. . .to Visible!

Isn't it interesting to think that God created the heavens and the earth just by speaking them into existence? He's pretty good at making something out of nothing. And the very things He created—the rocks, rivers, trees, and so forth—sing His praises! Best of all, He created all of those things. . .for us!

Only God can perform miracles. And though we can't see Him, we know that He is there, working them every day in our lives.

It takes a lot of faith to believe in a God we can't see, but when we look around at this beautiful planet (which He created for our enjoyment), it's easy to tell He's an awesome, miracle-working God! Praise Him!

What are your thoughts on God's creation?

....

....

....

....

....

....

....

....

....

....

....

....

....

....

....

....

....

Through faith we understand that the world was made by the Word of God. Things we see were made from what could not be seen.
HEBREWS 11:3

Who Am I?

We all have an identity. This means that certain personality traits, and other things that are unique only to you, have set you apart from other people. If you were asked to describe yourself, what would you say? As believers, our desire should be for others to see Christ in us and identify us by His presence in our lives.

Unbelievers often try to get Christians to take their eyes off Jesus to focus on worldly things that are used to create worldly identities. They want you to focus on your appearance, your popularity, your talents. . . But take care to guard yourself from that trap. Know who you are by knowing who He is. Let Jesus' love and His life show you who you are in Him.

Describe who you are—because of Jesus.

....

....

....

....

....

....

....

....

....

....

....

....

....

....

....

Christ gave you the Holy Spirit and He lives in you. You do not need anyone to teach you. The Holy Spirit is able to teach you all things. What He teaches you is truth and not a lie. Live by the help of Christ as the Holy Spirit has taught you.
1 JOHN 2:27

The Right Way Out

The Bible tells us that everyone experiences temptation. *Everyone* sins and struggles with the temptation to do something wrong. But God promises that whenever you are tempted to sin, He will *always* provide the right way out! Isn't that cool?

Have you ever looked for the way out before? The next time you're tempted to do something wrong. . .stop and ask God for the right way out and then look for it! Maybe your phone will ring right when you are tempted to watch a Netflix show that you know isn't a good choice. Or maybe God will help you remember the answer when you are tempted to cheat on a test. God will surprise you with the right way out—just don't forget to look for it!

What are some ways you can avoid temptation?

Your ears will hear a word behind you, saying, "This is the way, walk in it," whenever you turn to the right or to the left.
ISAIAH 30:21

Decorating Your Heart

Some women spend a lot of time and effort finding big pieces of costume jewelry that cost very little, but look very much like the real thing. It would be much better if they thought more about decorating from the inside, dressing up the heart, than about the outside with junk that will fade away.

Jesus wants girls to be decent and modest. He wants your inner beauty to be more important to you than your outward appearance. It matters more to Him how you treat others and how you live for Him. He doesn't care about your hairstyle or your fancy clothes. So work on letting the Holy Spirit grow you from the inside out instead!

What kind of beauty does Jesus care about?

....

....

....

....

....

....

....

....

....

....

....

....

....

....

....

....

....

Christian women should not be dressed in the kind of clothes and their hair should not be combed in a way that will make people look at them. They should not wear much gold or pearls or clothes that cost much money.
1 TIMOTHY 2:9

Need a Rest?

If you're exhausted from trying to say and do the right thing all of the time so that your friends will like you, you need a rest! If you're one of those people who never share your true feelings with anyone and bottle everything up inside because you're afraid your friends won't accept you as you are, you need a rest! If you're just plain tired of trying to live up to everyone's expectations, then you need a rest!

Jesus wants you to come to Him and be real. He wants you to be who He created you to be. You can be yourself in the presence of your heavenly Father. He wants to know how you are feeling about everything, and He loves you and accepts you no matter what—just as you are! Lay down all of your burdens at the feet of Jesus and curl up for a long rest in His loving arms.

How does it feel knowing you can share anything and everything with Jesus?

....

....

....

....

....

....

....

....

....

....

....

....

....

....

....

....

....

....

....

....

"Come to Me, all of you who work and have heavy loads. I will give you rest."
MATTHEW 11:28

Believing the Impossible

Have you ever faced a huge obstacle—one so big you couldn't see around it? You couldn't climb over it?

There's a really cool story in the Bible about some huge walls surrounding a town called Jericho. The people of God marched around those walls for seven days, and guess what happened. . .the walls fell down!

What if we prayed the walls down in our lives? If we looked beyond our limitations and saw ourselves the same way God sees us? If we refused to give up when things went wrong? If we prayed in faith?

The next time you're going through a really hard time, remember that God is a God of the impossible! (That's right—the Bible says He delights in doing the impossible!) So, even if you're facing a huge obstacle, choose to believe. . .and watch those walls come tumbling down!

Do you believe in the impossible? Why or why not?

....

....

....

....

....

....

....

....

....

....

....

....

....

....

....

....

....

Because the Jews had faith, the
walls of the city of Jericho fell
down after the Jews had walked
around the city for seven days.
HEBREWS 11:30

Nothing but the Truth

Your best friend wants you to tell a little white lie. Okay, not even a little white lie exactly—just not the whole truth.

But you know deep down exactly what your half-truth would do. It would disappoint not only your parents, but God too. And to disappoint your parents and God would hurt them. You'd not only let them down, but you'd break the trust that you've worked so hard to build up.

When the temptation comes to leave out parts of the truth, remember that even half-truths can hurt others. Ask God for His wisdom when you have important decisions to make. He won't ever lead you in the wrong direction—guaranteed!

What's wrong with telling a half-truth?

So stop lying to each other.
Tell the truth. . . . We all
belong to the same body.
EPHESIANS 4:25

Your Wish Is My Command

Once upon a time, a young man found a magic lamp. When he rubbed it, a genie appeared in a puff of smoke and offered the lad three wishes. He could have anything he wanted simply by asking for it.

As a child of God, you have something far better than a genie. You have a heavenly Father who has the power to give you anything you ask for. As the Owner of the universe, it's not at all difficult for Him to reach into His vast treasure house and grant your wishes. But unlike the genie in the lamp, God has *your* best interest in mind. That means He won't give you anything that would be bad for you, no matter how much you think you want it.

Don't be shy about asking God for the things you want. Rest assured that as long as what you're asking for is good for you, sooner or later it will come to pass.

Are you shy about asking God for things you want? Why or why not?

....

....

....

....

....

....

....

....

....

....

....

....

....

....

....

....

....

....

....

*"All things you ask for in prayer,
you will receive if you have faith."*
MATTHEW 21:22

More Great Books for Unique Girls Like You!

100 Extraordinary Stories for Courageous Girls

Girls are world-changers! And this deeply inspiring story-book proves it! This collection of 100 extraordinary stories of women of faith—from the Bible, history, and today—will empower you to know and understand how women have made a difference in the world and how much smaller our faith (and the biblical record) would be without them.

Hardback / 978-1-68322-748-9 / $16.99

Cards of Kindness for Courageous Girls: Shareable Devotions and Inspiration

You will delight in spreading kindness and inspiration wherever you go with these shareable *Cards of Kindness!* Each perforated page features a just-right-sized devotional reading plus a positive life message that will both uplift and inspire your young heart.

Paperback / 978-1-64352-164-0 / $7.99

With your parent's permission, check out **CourageousGirls.com** where you'll discover additional positive, faith-building activities and resources!

BARBOUR
kidz